# I've Passed, and So Will You.

Ishi Sharma

BookLeaf Publishing

India | USA | UK

Presentation by *BookLeaf Publishing*

Web: www.bookleafpub.com

E-mail: info@bookleafpub.com

ISBN: 9789360943837

First edition 2024

# Prologue

"Tell me a story,"
she said.
"Tell me a story from the very beginning."

I have never been much of a narrator,
and never been one to refuse Her, (no one is)
so I share with Her, from the very beginning,
the celestial soup that tightened and spun,
wound and grew, dipped and flew,
painted the night with one deft stroke,
illuminated forgetfully, leaving crumbs of light
in its wake.
A galaxy,
beyond yonder,
gleaming with the blaring light
of millions of stars and smiles and deaths and
stories and-

Oh. That's not what you meant?
Then I will start
smaller.

# Curiosity Killed the Birds

A smoky haze fills the yawning lens
of a dusty pair of rose-tinted glasses.
Setting them upon your nose,
its bridge might become wooden, spanning over
the mosquito infested water
that your pet is compelled to bathe in.
And that bridge might extend into the park
where you engage with the spinning
contraption for hours, belly aching from laughter
too rowdy to contain.
The bridge might connect to the pavilion, a
ceiling pattern of crossbars as messily arranged
as your thoughts, crossbars that you remember
once held bird nests
but now hold spikes.
Whatever happened to those birds?

# It's the First Day of School

When something is far off,
Time has got a way of
twirling her silky straight blonde hair
and licking her red apple lips
and gazing at you with her ocher eyes
and singing in her siren voice,
and patting your back with honey hands
and making that thing you musn't forget,
Forgettable.

When something is far off it prowls in the tall
grass of your memory,
eyes set with deadly precision on the time to
strike,
waiting to pounce until,
"Oh, look, it's August 31st!"
and it's upon you.

Before you know it you are
walking to those double doors together and
going in
alone?

# Let's Play a Game

When the music starts,
it's time to circle.

You don't know who made the rules of this
game,
But your heart starts and stops with the music
and the game fills the space in your mind with
tension,
coiling your thoughts and tightening your
muscles.

It fills the space so completely, so exhaustively.
It distracts so vigorously, so seductively
that you almost don't think of
what could be lying at the center of the circle,
and
How come
no one
ever speaks about it?

# Kids Often Fall on The Playground

You don't understand why,
when they could choose to walk,
they
always
run.

But even more fascinating:
Not all who run,
fall.

You know him, and he's naughty (surely he
deserves the sting of the concrete)
You know her, and she's rude (surely she
deserves it, too)
But there are others,
and when their blood splatters the concrete,
you cannot seem to justify
the retribution.

How does She decide who
runs
and who
falls?

# The Lyrics To That One Song

There's one song
you thoroughly enjoy.
The best song in existence.

It's got an infectious rhythm
and a glorious melody.
Perhaps a guitar strumming softly in the backing
track
among the other great-song things.

This is a special song (or so you've been told)
and the only one you know.
And songs like these
come once
and never
Return.

You knew the reason at one point (you'd been
told)
but it appears to have slipped your mind.
If only you could understand the words
you wouldn't be left wondering
Why is it so special, again?

# You've Got Three Wishes

There are no restrictions on what you may wish.
Three wishes, one you.
Many ways to go about it.

The first for some sort of superpower.
The second for a favorite snack.
The third stowed away for later.

But really that's only a precaution,
because why would you ever need
another wish?

# Never Stayed Up This Late

It's amazing how complex a white ceiling can
become
when it transforms into a canvas for thoughts
Much bigger than you.

As the hours file begrudgingly past,
your thoughts consolidate into one.
This one thought, he bears an
ugly stature,
clumsy balance,
and the name of "Death".

He can murmur for hours on end,
yet somehow is always
interrupting
something or the other.
He'll stubbornly sit at the forefront of your
mind,
nagging rudely until you
acknowledge him.
.

Before he lets you sleep,
he yanks a single tear from your eye,
letting gravity do the work as it rolls down the
side of your cheek

to make a miniscule splash on the mattress cover
below.
The small droplet leaves an even tinier spot,
which dries in only a matter of seconds.
It's in this moment which you understand,
the droplet
cannot
roll
back.

# It's the Next Morning

And you feel fine.
Good, even.

Until you remember he's nocturnal,
and will be back for more
when the night falls.
How to prepare for his arrival?

# A Fact About Death

About 155,000 people die every day.

He's a busy man.

# The Ants You Stepped On

On your way to school
were unsuspecting.
Time did to them
what she did to you.

Death,
characteristically rude,
was not so tactful.
He barged in as if
they were
ready.

And you
held Her power in your hands.
Is this what She does
all
the
Time?

# Another Fact About Death

The remains of your body will smell sweet as it ages.

Time's doing.

# Your Second Aunt on Your Father's Side

Just recently
"passed".

Passed on to a different place.
Passively allowed herself to be taken by
him.

Became part of your past.

# The Third Wish

What's so interesting about regret,
is that you often regret engaging in regret.
But by then it's too late,
and here comes Time with another wave of
Regret.

In this way,
despair over what is past
is like despair over what is yet to come.

The third wish, stowed for later,
is to live,
and never leave,
the moment in which
he arrives.

# The Doomsday Clock

You learn of the doomsday clock
in your history class
at the ripe age
of 18-years-old.

Time will tell you,
your clock knew of you long before then.

Tick,
Tock,
Tick,
Tock.
Stop.

# Your Last Words Were Not Significant

And neither were you.

# A Final Fact About Death

You remain conscious up to twenty seconds post-death.

…19, 20.

# He's Arrived

You'll be pleased to know
that this story does have a culmination.
He came and went just as I suspected he would,
swift and clean,
no pain.
Not for me at least.

All that worry,
for nothing but the
stopping
of a
clock.